CREATED FOR SOMEONE

For this reason a man will leave his father and mother and be joined to his wife, and the two will become one flesh. This mystery is profound, but I am talking about Christ and the church.

~Ephesians 5:31–32

CREATED FOR SOMEONE

WHAT THE BIBLE SAYS ABOUT MARRIAGE

MARIO VILLELLA

WordCrafts Press

Created for Someone
Copyright © 2025
Mario Villella

Paperback ISBN: 978-1-962218-96-2

Published by WordCrafts Press
Cody, Wyoming 82414
www.wordcrafts.net

CONTENTS

Introduction

*T*his book is the third in a series that began *Working Your Way Through Life* and *It Takes Two to Tangle*. I am following the format and pattern of those books by breaking down a topic into multiple easy-to-read chapters, with an expectation that the book would be read a little bit each day, (although I admit, these books are also pretty easy to read all in one sitting, too). Just as with the other two books, many of these ideas were originally delivered verbally in sermons at Good News Church in Ocala, Florida.

While this book will probably be most helpful to married people (since they could begin applying these truths immediately to the marriage they are already in) I would say this book wouldn't be a waste of time for unmarried people to read. It's not a long read, and several of the chapters were written with single people in view. Additionally, there are many unmarried people who *will be married* one day in the future, and it does not hurt to know what the Bible says before you get there. In fact, most married people who learn helpful things about marriage wish they had learned it earlier than they did.

So whether you need some pre-marital counsel, or some assistance with a marriage on the rocks, or perhaps something in between, I hope this book is helpful to you. May God's message within it (there's a lot of Bible in here) bring you hope or joy or wisdom, or even be the first step in having a connection with the God who created you.

Who Does Marriage Exist For?
And Who Created It?

"For in bringing many sons to glory, it was entirely appropriate that God—all things exist for Him and through Him—should make the source of their salvation perfect through sufferings."
~Hebrews 2:10

"He is the image of the invisible God, the firstborn over all creation. For everything was created by Him in heaven and on earth, the visible and the invisible, whether thrones or dominions or rulers or authorities— all things have been created through Him and for Him."
~Colossians 1:15–16

Let's begin with the first question in the chapter title: Who does marriage exist for? It is an important question, but one that is not often asked. And I would guess the most popular answer is mostly assumed: *for the people in the marriage.* I think it is fair to say most people seem to live, act, and believe their marriages exist for themselves.

In light of that, I thought it would be helpful to start this book off with a challenge to one of our most basic understandings of marriage. What if your marriage didn't exist *for you?*

In contrast to mainstream culture, the assumption of the Bible is that marriage exists *for God.* This is easy to ascertain because the Bible makes the much broader statement that *everything* exists for God. If you look back at Hebrews 2:10, you'll see it right there in the eight words that come right after the word "God." Right in the middle of a sentence about why God ordained that Jesus should die on the cross is an explanatory (almost parenthetical) statement that is echoed in other places in the Bible: *"all things exist for Him and through Him."*

The second passage printed at the start of this chapter (Col. 1:15–16) is quite similar. Again, it is a sentence that is part of a larger section about the relationship between Jesus and God the Father. However, at the end of the verse, you find almost the exact same truth the writer of Hebrews mentioned: all things were made by Him and for Him.

The wording here is slightly different in that it says that all things were *created* by Him and for Him, instead saying that they *exist* by Him and for Him. But the effect is the same. It is a strong declaration about where everything came from and what everything exists for.

However, there is another difference between the two passages. The one from Hebrews was speaking about the Father, and the passage from Colossians is about the Son. (You can verify this by reading those verses in context where the words "Father" and "Son" are used in the surrounding verses to describe the persons being talked about.)

It is interesting, and has long been noted by Christians, that the Bible credits the creation of the world to both the

Father and the Son (Jesus Christ). This could be confusing for people who do not understand the doctrine of the Trinity—"Wait a minute. Who made the world? God or Jesus?" To that, the Christian replies: both. We believe Jesus and the Father are the same God, and yet referred to as different persons. Feel free to grab a book on the Trinity if you want to know more about this, but I'd like to get back to the topic of marriage at this time.

Today's scripture passages teach that everything was created by Jesus and for Jesus, and that everything exists by God and for God.

So, as strange as it may sound, that's where we begin our teaching on marriage: Marriage, like every other created thing, exists for God/Jesus. Yes, that's pretty basic, but basic truths are good places to start. (It reminds me of how the famous coach Vince Lombardi began his NFL training camp with the words, "This is a football.") Before we get into any of the details, it is good to begin with the foundational truth that will guide how we interpret and apply all of the other things we find in the Bible about marriage.

And before you think, "This is a little too basic. How can pondering such an abstract truth actually help me with the way I live my life?" Let me ask you to think it through. Can you imagine the difference between the couples who believe their marriages exist for God versus the couples who believe their marriages exist for themselves? It's not just philosophy; those two beliefs will actually create two different marriages, won't they?

Prayer: *God, I acknowledge all marriages exist for You. Jesus, I acknowledge You created all things, visible and invisible. Thank You for creating me. Help me to live according to Your will for Your creation and not by my own will.*

Marriage Is A Reflection Of Something Else

*"In the same way, husbands are to love their wives
as their own bodies. He who loves his wife loves himself.
For no one ever hates his own flesh but provides and
cares for it, just as Christ does for the church, since we
are members of His body. For this reason a man will
leave his father and mother and be joined to his wife,
and the two will become one flesh. This mystery is profound, but I am talking about Christ and the church.
To sum up, each one of you is to love his wife as himself,
and the wife is to respect her husband."*
~Ephesians 5:28–33

*H*aving established some basics, today we move on to
Bible verses that actually use the words "husband" and "wife"—
verses that are more specifically and pointedly about marriage.

Today's passage is from Ephesians 5, which is possibly
the most famous chapter in the Bible regarding the topic of
marriage. (I think I have heard more marriage sermons from
Ephesians 5 than any other portion of Scripture.)

There is a lot to say about the verses in this chapter—
and we will return to Ephesians 5 a few more times over the
course of this book—but for now, I wanted to simply point

out some more foundational truths that are assumed about marriage in the scriptures.

This passage shows marriage does not exist separate from everything else, but was apparently made to mirror another greater relationship. In this passage, as the author (the Apostle Paul) describes how husbands are to love their wives, he connects the whole concept to Christ and the church. Notice how the husband's role of providing and caring is compared to how Jesus provided and cares for His congregation of people.

Also in this section, Paul quotes what is perhaps the most well-known Old Testament passage about marriage, Genesis 2:24. It's the part that says: *"For this reason a man will leave his father and mother and be joined to his wife, and the two will become one flesh."* That verse is definitely about marriage (it was originally found in the middle of the Adam and Eve story) and yet Paul immediately follows it up with a statement about how he is, somehow, talking about the union between Christ and His church.

For now, let me point out that if marriage is supposed to mirror the relationship Jesus Christ has with His people, then, at the very least, this means we don't just get to make up our own rules about it and govern it however we want. Marriage is something that is supposed to look and be a particular way, as prescribed by the Creator of it.

This is important, as many of us live in a society where it is assumed that marriage is this somewhat malleable thing that can be flexed in order to match our cultural expectations and personal preferences. We both make and remove rules about it. We declare it will be this way or that. But all along, there is a Creator who designed it to be a reflection of a something specific He has in mind.

Prayer: *Heavenly Father, thank You for caring for Your people. May my (future or current) marriage be a reflection of the good news of Jesus Christ, rather than it merely being a reflection of my own personal desires.*

Day 3

Marriage Is Union

"This is why a man leaves his father and mother and bonds with his wife and they become one flesh."
~Genesis 2:24

I mentioned previously, Genesis 2:24 is perhaps the most well-known Old Testament passage about marriage. I heard it referenced the other day when I was watching an old rerun of the TV show *Everybody Loves Raymond*. Many people are aware of this Bible passage which says marriage is when two people become one.

One reason this verse has had such profound influence would be because of the number of times it is quoted in the New Testament (Matt. 19:5, Mark 10:6, Eph. 5:31, and 1 Cor. 6:16). To my knowledge, there isn't any other verse on marriage that gets repeated in the Bible more often than this one.

So, let's take a look at it, shall we?

If you were to read the verses just before and after it, you'd quickly see this verse (as mentioned on Day 2 of this book) is right in the middle of the Adam and Eve story. And yet, the verse sticks out in an unusual way in that it's not about Adam and Eve.

The story of Adam's relationship to Eve begins with God talking about her in Genesis 2:18 and then God actually making her in 2:22. However, the narrator of that story pulls back from talking about Adam and Eve for just one verse (today's scripture: Genesis 2:24) to make a point about marriage.

The fact that this verse isn't about Adam is obvious enough in that it describes a man leaving his father and mother to create a new family with a woman. Adam had no earthly parents (that is quite clear in the preceding story), and this is therefore a biblical teaching, not about Adam and Eve, but about all of the marriages that would follow theirs.

And what is the point? Simply that marriage involves a man leaving the family unit he grew up in (and the woman doing the same) and the two of them joining together to create a brand-new family unit that didn't exist before that moment.

Marriage is set apart from other relationships (like friendships, parenthood, or sibling relationships) in that it somehow takes two people who were previously unrelated and "bonds" them into a new thing that comes into existence at their joining. Many people simply take this for granted, but it is amazing to think about.

Understanding this will be a major building block for understanding other things the Bible says about marriage. For instance, why does the Bible limit sexual acts to marriage, when those acts could clearly be accomplished by unmarried people? Could it be that sex is a kind of "bonding" that matches the marriage relationship? Or, as another example, why does the Bible forbid divorce in most cases, while saying so little about the ending of friendships? Could it be the bonding of marriage creates different obligations than the friendship commitment? We will get to these topics as we go along.

For now, let's notice that right at the beginning of the Bible we see the nature of marriage is to unite two previously non-united things. Pondering this truth should lead us to all sorts of interesting conversations about what united people ought to do that is different from non-united people. Should they live in separate homes? Should they keep their finances separate with her paying her bills and him paying his? Should they keep secrets from one another because a husband's life choices aren't any of his wife's business? And vice-versa?

I believe the more we learn about God's perspective on marriage the easier it is to answer these questions.

Prayer: *Almighty Creator, help me to understand the implications and applications that come along with the truth You gave us when You told us "they become one flesh."*

MARRIAGE IS ABOUT CO-WORKERSHIP

"The Lord God took the man and placed him in the garden of Eden to work it and watch over it. And the Lord God commanded the man, 'You are free to eat from any tree of the garden, but you must not eat from the tree of the knowledge of good and evil, for on the day you eat from it, you will certainly die.' Then the Lord God said, 'It is not good for the man to be alone. I will make a helper as his complement.'"

~Genesis 2:15–18

While we are in the book of Genesis, it will be helpful to look back at the verses that come just before God created Eve for Adam. These verses give us some insight about what God was thinking when He made the first wife for the first husband.

Firstly notice, after creating Adam, God says, *"It is not good for the man to be alone."* Most of the sermons I have heard about this text have involved the preacher pointing out the importance of companionship. They often seemed to take the phrase, "It is not good for the man to be *alone*," to mean something like, "It is not good for the man to be *lonely*."

Sure, I don't have a problem believing God was

concerned about Adam's well-being and therefore wanted to create a companion to alleviate his loneliness. However, I believe there is more to it than just that. Upon further investigation it sure seems that God thought that Adam was going find Eve to be helpful for something. What was it?

In this passage God says: "*I will make a helper as his complement.*" The word complement (which is not the same word as "compliment") is sometimes translated "suitable for him" and comes from a Hebrew word sometimes translated "opposite." I think it is similar to the way we use the term "complementary colors" in art class; they are colors (opposite from each other on the color wheel) that go together.

It also seems significant that the word "helper" is used to describe what Eve is to be to Adam. Obviously "helper" is not exactly the same thing as "companion." The way it comes across is almost as if some kind of task would need to be accomplished by the two of them. And that makes sense because the preceding verses said God had put Adam in the garden "to work it."

Additionally, God had given Adam a specific command to obey. Perhaps part of Eve's job was for her to help Adam do the garden work God had assigned to him and/or obey the command God had given to him?

At the very least, we can know part of Eve's role as Adam's complement was to enable him to bring new people into the world. Though I haven't mentioned it yet, earlier in Genesis it was declared God "*created them male and female,*" and shortly after that God said, "*Be fruitful and multiply, fill the earth, and subdue it.*" Filling the earth with people is a big job, and Adam certainly couldn't have done that alone. This makes me think a huge part of the reason God created Eve for Adam was because she was sexually suitable for him. After all, if God only cared about alleviating Adam's loneliness, He could have created another man. Something more was at stake.

So, I have often told my congregation that marriage isn't only about companionship. It is a co-workership. God gave Adam a job to do, and then gave him a helper to do it with. Similarly, in our marriages we should consider not only, "How might he make me feel less lonely?" or "How might she alleviate my unhappiness?" but more importantly: "What job might God have for us to accomplish together that we couldn't do alone?"

Prayer: *Lord, I pray You would guide me and my (future or current) spouse so we would accomplish Your will together rather than as individuals.*

JESUS' BELIEFS ABOUT MARRIAGE
PART ONE

"Some Pharisees approached Him to test Him. They asked, 'Is it lawful for a man to divorce his wife on any grounds?'

'Haven't you read' he replied, 'that He who created them in the beginning made them male and female,' and He also said, 'For this reason a man will leave his father and mother and be joined to his wife and the two will become one flesh?'"

~Matthew 19:3–5

esus Christ is the Creator of the world according to Colossians 1:16. (We covered this back on day one of this book.) However, he also lived as a human being on this earth, and we have four biographies about him in the Bible (Matthew, Mark, Luke, and John). We are in the blessed position of being able to know what our Creator thinks about marriage, and we can even read the words He said about it during His lifetime here on earth.

It may be helpful to also note that Jesus was an unmarried man. And as far as we can tell from the sources we have, Jesus didn't have a lot of official teaching on the topic of marriage. He acknowledged (in today's passage) there were already truths deposited in the Hebrew Scriptures about this topic, and He also allowed His Apostles to teach more about it after His death, resurrection, and ascension. But it is safe to say Jesus didn't teach on this topic extensively.

However, that is not to say He didn't address this topic at all. Not only did Jesus cover the topic of marriage in the Sermon on the Mount, but His most extended teaching comes from the occasion (above) where the Pharisees asked him about divorce.

We will revisit some of these verses in tomorrow's reading, but for today I wanted to point out Jesus made an assumption about marriage (an assumption most people have made throughout history) that is often no longer made in the Western world: Marriage is a male-female arrangement.

Now this assumption would have been made by Jesus' questioners as well. Notice they asked him "*Is it lawful for a man to divorce his wife on any grounds?*" They assumed marriage was something between a man and a woman. And Jesus backed up their assumption by quoting the first page of the Bible: "*He who created them in the beginning made them male and female.*"

What is interesting to me is this quotation wasn't really the verse Jesus needed in order to make his main point (which we will get to on Day 6). The primary passage Jesus used to answer their question about divorce was the "two-become-one passage" (that we already covered on Day 3) which is from Genesis 2:24. However, before Jesus quoted that passage, he quoted another passage (one that doesn't explicitly mention marriage) which comes 28 verses earlier. He quotes that God made them *"male and female"* and applies that to the topic of marriage.

I've heard it said Jesus never addressed the topic of gay marriage. But this is barely and only technically true. As we can see from the passage above, Jesus didn't need to address what we call "gay marriage." Jesus assumed marriage is a male-female arrangement and quoted the Bible that way.

Prayer: *Lord, if You are truly the Creator, You have the right to define marriage however You see fit. Please help me to see things the way You see them.*

Jesus' Beliefs About Marriage
Part Two

"So they are no longer two, but one flesh. Therefore, what God has joined together, man must not separate."
~Matthew 19:6

This is the next verse that comes right after the verses we looked at on Day 5. After Jesus quoted *"the two will become one flesh"* from Genesis, He said these words that we have set aside as today's Scripture.

Remember, the reason Jesus was speaking was He was answering a question about divorce. The Pharisees were essentially asking him about how long a marriage was supposed to last. They said, *"Is it lawful for a man to divorce his wife on any grounds?"*

This was a somewhat controversial issue during Jesus' day. There were at least two schools of (Jewish) thought regarding this topic: the most famous ones being named Hillel and Shammai. One of these groups was more conservative than the other, and the Pharisees may have wondered which side Jesus was on. They may have even been hoping that in getting him to take a side they could anger the followers of the other side and get them to oppose Jesus.

(Note: this kind of trapping was something they did; see Mark 12:13)

Whatever their motive, Jesus answered the question by declaring from the Hebrew Scriptures that marriage is a union. He obviously believes it to be a male-female union. And, in today's passage, it's clear He believes it is a *permanent* union.

Jesus answered their question by quoting Genesis 2:24 about a man being *"joined to his wife"* and then followed up with this instruction: *"What God has joined together, man must not separate."*

This teaching is a general command against divorce.

Note: The reason I included the qualifier "general" is because the next thing Jesus says in the verses that follow (Matthew 16:7–9) seem to speak of an exception to the ordinary rule against divorce—sexual immorality. This "exception clause" (as it has been referred to over the years), as well as the words of the Apostle Paul in 1 Corinthians 7:15, has given many Christians reason to believe, while God forbids divorce generally, He also acknowledges a few specific exceptions where a person may be no longer bound to their spouse.

Okay, back to our passage. Please notice Jesus not only believes a man and woman are "joined" together, but He also has some specific beliefs about *who* did the joining. Jesus said we should not separate what *God* has joined together.

This is helpful to know, especially if we encounter the

common belief: "Well, I can divorce my wife because I'm allowed to undo any choices I made." Or, "Since I am the one who chose to unite with my husband, I can choose to un-unite with him."

No. Looking at Jesus' words, we see the reason we don't (generally speaking) get to decide to divorce is because we aren't the ones who did the joining. God did.

So, even while acknowledging some marriages end because of the unrepentant sins of adultery and/or abandonment, we can clearly see Jesus believes marriage is supposed to be a permanent union.

Prayer: *Jesus, I pray I would take marriage vows as seriously as You take them.*

MARRIAGE SHOULD BE CHARACTERIZED BY LOVE

"In the same way, husbands are to love their wives as their own bodies. He who loves his wife loves himself. For no one ever hates his own flesh but provides and cares for it, just as Christ does for the church since we are members of his body.

~Ephesians 5:28–30

[Older women] are to teach what is good so they may encourage the young women to love their husbands and to love their children.

~Titus 2:3b–4

*H*usbands and wives are supposed to love each other. This is not counter-cultural. In fact, this is one of the few areas where the Bible and our culture (I'm referring to the United States) overlap. It is simply taken for granted that husbands and wives are supposed to love each other. I'm not so sure that was always a given in the society that the New Testament was first written in.

You can search the internet and quickly find historical information that includes the idea that Roman Empire-era relationships often included marriages that were non-romantic and not characterized by love and faithfulness.

Roman Empire marriages were often the strategic merging of two families (arranged by parents) for financial and social reasons. People in that era may have ended up marrying people they didn't particularly like. Men in that era were not always expected to be sexually faithful to the woman they married.

It's helpful to realize it was in the midst of *that* kind of society the Bible instructed husbands to love their wives. In fact, it doesn't simply say that they are to love them, but to love them in the same way they love themselves. Notice our verse today reads: *husbands are to love their wives as their own bodies... for no one ever hates his own flesh but provides and cares for it."*

Though our culture may not need to be reminded that husbands ought to love their wives, in the midst of all of the unfaithfulness and unkindness we see in the marriages of our day, it is a good reminder that God calls husbands to love their wives the same amount and in the same way they love themselves. Not only should a husband never harm his wife (just as he doesn't enjoy harm coming his way) a husband shouldn't be selfish, putting his needs above hers.

I also included the section from the book of Titus in today's reading to be sure it is apparent this love is to be a two-way street. The Bible famously tells husbands to love their wives on multiple occasions (more times than it tells wives to love their husbands!)

However, it is not as if wives aren't supposed to love their husbands as well. The verse from Titus (above) shows the older women in a Christian congregation were supposed to teach the younger women to love their husbands (and children).

In fact, it is interesting and helpful to notice that love can, in some way, be taught. We tend to think love is such a romantic and uncontrollable thing that we might assume that a woman wouldn't ever even need to be taught how to love her husband. "It just comes naturally," we might say. Yeah, well, maybe. But apparently it can diminish over time and needs to be "encouraged" even by other people who are outside of the marriage (in the case in Titus it was older women helping younger women).

So, even though we all know married people ought to love each other, I thought it worth one chapter of this book to remember the Bible says so. And it said this even during a time when that wasn't a given.

Prayer: *Father, I pray You would teach me to love the way I should. Perhaps You would even provide other people in my life who would encourage me to love others (especially and including my spouse) the way I love myself. And may I encourage those around me in that way, too.*

Day 8

We Have Some Measure Of Control Over Our Feelings

"…Everyone must be quick to hear, slow to speak, and slow to anger."

~James 1:19b

"Don't worry about anything, but in everything, through prayer and petition, with thanksgiving, let your requests be made known to God."

~Philippians 4:6

"Rejoice in the Lord always. I will say it again: Rejoice!"

~Philippians 4:4

You have some measure of control over your feelings. This is something the Bible doesn't say explicitly, but rather seems to be something that is *assumed* all over the Bible. For that reason, I included multiple scriptures for today's reading. There are far more than three places in the Bible that say this kind of thing, but I figured these three verses would suffice.

When James told his readers to be "*slow to anger,*" it's

because he believed they had the ability to do that. It's almost as if humans have invisible knobs and can somewhat control how fast or slow they blow up about something.

When Paul told people not to worry but rather to pray, it must have been because people have some kind of control over how much they freak out about a particular concern. Even when Paul told the Philippians to "*Rejoice in the Lord*" he was telling them to "be happy about Jesus." (We don't often use the word "rejoice," and so we may think this was just some sort of weird religious instruction and not notice he was teaching them to *feel* a certain way about their Lord.)

The reason I am bringing this up is because we live in a time where many people act as if we are almost slaves to our feelings. We certainly see that idea applied to romantic feelings. Elvis had a hit song (that I still hear at every wedding reception I attend) with the chorus that insists he can't help but fall in love with his girlfriend. But even in non-romantic situations, we often hear people say things like "I can't help but be mad about this" or "this situation has totally stressed me out" in ways that imply we cannot choose how angry we get or how much we worry. We tend to believe emotions are things that merely happen *to us* involuntarily, and we have no control over them.

The verses we read today (and many others) don't come from that kind of thinking.

To be clear, emotions are often overwhelming. And I'm quite sure God knows that, because overwhelming emotions are spoken about in the Bible (see Mark 14:34 or Psalm 61:2 for examples). There may be feelings that are difficult—and perhaps, at times, even impossible—to completely quench in certain situations. Therefore, I am not even trying to make the case that we have 100% control over all of our emotional impulses. At this point, I'm merely trying to say the Bible assumes that we don't have 0% control over them.

Why is this important? And what does this have to do with marriage?

This is important because if we think loving, forgiving, calming down, and putting away bitterness are things completely outside of our control, we may think obeying the Bible in these areas is outside of our control.

Additionally, when we see (later in this book) the Bible teach against things like getting involved in a spiritual mismatch (ex: a Christian marrying a Buddhist) we may think: "I can't help who I fall in love with." In that case, we might be dismissing God's word and instead adopting the worldview of an Elvis song.

Prayer: *Lord, thank You for giving me some control over my own life. I pray I would feel the way You want me to feel. Further, I pray I would take responsibility, as much as I can, for the emotions in my life. Help me to use them in ways that honor You.*

THE BIBLE (AND GOD) TELLS US WHO
AND HOW TO LOVE

"Husbands love your wives just as Christ loved the church and gave Himself for her…"
~Ephesians 5:25

"[Older women] are to teach what is good so they may encourage the young women to love their husbands and to love their children.
~Titus 2:3b–4

"You have heard it said, 'Love your neighbor' and hate your enemy. But I tell you, love your enemies and pray for those who persecute you…"
~Matthew 5:43–44

*T*oday's topic is another one that is implied by many scriptures all throughout the Bible and therefore it is worth looking at multiples passages to see the connections.

Yesterday's concept might be helpful to remember today: we have some measure of control regarding our feelings. God has every right to command us to love our spouses. We are to obey Him and love whoever He says to love.

Having said that, sometimes I wonder if "love" is somewhat different than other emotions. There are times when the Bible speaks of love more like it is an *action* than it is a *feeling*. Biblical love often seems to be something like "do what is best for the other person regardless of how you feel." This might be most easy to see in the words Jesus spoke in Matthew 5: "*Love your enemies.*"

Has anyone ever "fallen in love" with their enemies? This command involves choosing to not hold your enemies' hostility against them, but rather that you would bless those people who deserve to be cursed. I am not sure Jesus was also requiring that we have "happy feelings of affection" toward our enemies when He said this. Perhaps that is what He meant, but I'm not certain of it. After all, Romans 12:17–20 also addresses a similar topic, and the command there seems to be to *do good* for your enemies far more than to *feel good* about them. (On the other hand, 1 Corinthians 13:3 says one can *do good* apart from love, and if that happens, it is worthless.)

So, love is a tough word to pin down sometimes. But, either way, we can be certain about this: love clearly involves doing good toward its object, and God has the right to tell us to love whoever He wants us to love. Therefore, the verses that tell us to love our spouse truly are commands we can and should obey.

Prayer: *Father, I want to submit to You and love who You call me to love, even in the cases where it is difficult.*

It Matters Who You Marry

"Do not intermarry with them. Do not give your daughters to their sons or take their daughters for your sons, because they will turn your sons away from Me to worship other gods. Then the Lord's anger will burn against you, and He will swiftly destroy you."

~Deuteronomy 7:3–4

"A wife is bound as long as her husband is living. But if her husband dies, she is free to be married to anyone she wants—only in the Lord."

~1 Corinthians 7:39

It matters who you marry. And there are a few places (see above) where the Bible warns that someone who worships the true God should not marry someone who doesn't.

The first of these two passages comes from the instructions given to the Israelites in the Old Testament. As they were taking over the land God had promised them, they were taught to not intermarry with the Hittites, Amorites, Canaanites, etc.

I think it is helpful to point out the reason given is not because God is against inter-ethnic marriage. The emphasis of the passage is clear that God is against *inter-faith* marriage. The reason God gave the Hebrews for not marrying a Girgashite is not because he or she had a different skin color or different physical traits. The passage says not to marry them *"because they will turn your sons away from Me to worship other gods."*

And I believe that principle would still apply today. I can't see why it would matter that a dark-skinned person marries a light-skinned person, or that a Pakistani woman might marry a Chinese guy. But, of course, it matters if you marry someone who turns you away from worshiping God.

The second passage above is from the New Testament and is an application of this principle (originally given to Israelites) but now applied to Christians.

The apostle Paul, in a chapter that gives all sorts of marriage instructions to single people, married people, widows, etc., teaches that once someone's spouse dies they are free to marry again to anyone they choose. (Paul actually uses female terms in this verse, saying a *wife* is free to remarry once her husband dies, but I see no reason not to assume this also applies to *husbands* whose wives have died.) And it is notable Paul puts one qualifier onto the *"anyone she wants"* portion of the verse. It's not simply *"anyone she wants"* but rather *"anyone she wants—only in the Lord."*

I see no other reasonable way to take this verse other than that Paul is teaching that after the death of a spouse, the remaining spouse is free to marry anyone they want as long as that person belongs to the Lord.

Given the reason for it, there is also no logical reason why this would only apply to *second* marriages. This teaching is consistent with the Lord's other concerns throughout the

Bible. If you are a follower of God, do not marry someone who will pull you away from following Him. If you are a follower of Christ, marry someone who is also devoted to Christ.

Prayer: *Lord, You are great and worthy to be worshiped. I acknowledge I need to factor that in, even to my marriage decisions.*

Avoiding A Spiritual Mismatch

"Do not be mismatched with unbelievers. For what partnership is there between righteousness and lawlessness? Or what fellowship does light have with darkness? What agreement does Christ have with Belial? Or what does a believer have in common with a unbeliever?"

~2 Corinthians 6:14–15

Though this particular verse is not specifically addressing dating or marriage, the principle outlined here is especially important toward this topic.

That verb, "mismatched," in the first sentence, is an English translation of a Greek word. Well, actually all of the words in this verse are; the New Testament was originally written in Greek and is translated into English for our convenience. Anyway, that word, "mismatched," can also be translated "unequally yoked." It's a compound word that involves both the word for "yoke" (which is an agricultural tool that joins together two animals for the purpose of plowing) and another word that means "of a different kind."

In this verse, the Apostle Paul was using an agricultural idea and applying the concept to human relationships. The agricultural part goes back at least to the time of Deuteron-omy where the Israelites were instructed to "*not plow with an ox and a donkey together.*"

There may be more to it than just this, but it seems there was a practical reason to avoid these kinds of farming mismatches. If one animal was significantly stronger or faster than the other, and yet they were bound together trying to complete the same task at the same time, it might mess up the whole operation.

With that imagery in mind, Paul tells the Christians in Corinth to not be mismatched or "unequally yoked" with unbelievers. He follows that up with a series of rhetorical questions showing that just like light and darkness don't mix, and just like Christ and Belial (probably a reference to a demon or Satan) don't mix, neither should believers be bound together with unbelievers.

As I said earlier, this isn't specifically a marriage verse. This idea might find its application in all sorts of other ways. I bet there have been many Christians who have gone down a dark road for a time because they allowed a close friendship with the wrong person to lead them astray. I can imagine there have been all sorts of ethical issues that rise up when a Christian and an unbeliever co-owned a business together. But I can't think of any kind of relationship on earth where this would be more important to apply than to the person you link up with for life.

Of course there have been many occasions where a Lutheran and a Hindu pledged their lives to one another, but can you see the pitfalls there? If someone heading east is tied to someone going west, it's going to frustrate both parties. And if someone who is aiming for God, is yoked to someone who is aiming toward another god, it is going to cause troubles.

If you remember back on Day 8 of this book, we learned we have some measure of control over our feelings. That chapter was written anticipating this one. Too many lovers say, "But I can't help the way I feel about him. I just have to marry him!" and then they enter into a spiritual mismatch this verse commands us to avoid. That earlier chapter was written to help us realize it is possible to obey this verse.

Of course, there are times when these kinds of mismatches can't be helped. After all, some people become Christians *after* they've already married a non-Christian. It is also possible two people claiming to be Christians can get married, only for one of them to later renounce their faith. These are unfortunate situations we will address in the next chapter. But, for now, today's teaching is: Don't knowingly get into a spiritual mismatch on purpose.

Prayer: *Lord, help me take seriously the direction I am heading because of You. And help me to take seriously anyone I might partner with, so they will help me continue in that direction and not take me off course.*

DAY 12

WHEN THE MISMATCH IS ALREADY IN PLACE

"But I (not the Lord) say to the rest: If any brother has an unbelieving wife and she is willing to live with him, he must not leave her. Also, if any woman has an unbelieving husband and he is willing to live with her, she must not leave her husband... But if the unbeliever leaves, let him leave. A brother or sister is not bound in such cases. God has called you to live in peace."
~1 Corinthians 7:12–13 & 15

$\mathcal{I}$ve included this passage because I think it's important to address what to do if you find yourself already in a spiritual mismatch. After reading yesterday's verses: *"Do not be mismatched with unbelievers. For what partnership is there between righteousness and lawlessness?"* I could imagine a Christian who is married to a non-Christian thinking that means he or she would be wise (or even obligated) to get a divorce. After all, believers aren't supposed to be partnered with unbelievers, right? Perhaps divorce is the only righteous way to deal with this problem?

Apparently not. Paul told the Corinthians not to leave an unbelieving spouse if that spouse is willing to remain in the marriage.

It is very likely there were several people in the city of Corinth who had become followers of Jesus Christ—however, when that happened, their spouse did not do the same. And perhaps, some of them thought divorce was their best option.

In fact, some of them might have even thought they were being spiritually polluted by being partnered with an unbeliever. You can picture it, can't you? Some lady goes to church every Sunday and is trying to live her life according to God's will. Meanwhile, her husband continues to worship idols down at the temple like he always had before. Maybe he even comes home one night cussing up a storm and/or singing the praises of Jupiter or Venus. And then Christian lady sleeps with him that night. Has she now been made dirty by this idol-worshiper?

Paul says, *no*. In fact, it's pretty much the opposite of that. In verse 14 (it's not in the quote above, but you can look it up) Paul says an *"unbelieving husband is set apart for God by the wife."* I don't know exactly what that means, but clearly Paul believed the Christian wife was having more of a positive spiritual effect on him than he was polluting her.

So the solution to a spiritual mismatch already in place is typically not divorce; it is faithfulness to the marriage.

However, Paul does point out an exception. And the exception is if the unbeliever initiates the divorce. In that case, the teaching is that the other spouse (who was not trying to end the marriage) is not doing anything wrong by being abandoned. In fact, in a lot of cases, that can't be stopped. People are going to do what they want to do. In that culture (and ours) there were probably plenty of instances where one spouse became a follower of Jesus, and the other spouse couldn't handle that. It may have felt like being married to a whole new person. And so they left. And Paul here says: "*A brother or sister is not bound in such cases.*"

In verse 12, Paul says this is his command and not the Lord's, but I don't think that means he didn't expect anyone to feel obligated to follow these instructions. I think he may have been saying something more like, "I'm not specifically quoting Jesus here." Overall, you can tell this messenger of the Lord believed Christian spouses should try to make it work out with their non-Christian partners if they could.

Prayer: *Lord, thank You for saving me. I pray You would use me to be a source of spiritual blessing even to the unbelievers in my family.*

SUBMISSION IN MARRIAGE
PART ONE

"...be filled by the Spirit... submitting to one another in the fear of Christ. Wives, submit to your own husbands as to the Lord, for the husband is the head of the wife as Christ is the head of the church. He is the Savior of the body. Now as the church submits to Christ, so wives are to submit to their husbands in everything. Husbands, love your wives, just as Christ loved the church and gave Himself for her."
~Ephesians 5:18b & 21–25

This is probably the most controversial Bible passage on the topic of marriage. I say that as an American in the 2020s. I have a feeling not every culture finds this passage to be off-putting, however many Americans are fairly sensitive (if not disgusted) by any suggestion of a woman submitting to a man.

Actually, that's not entirely true. If a woman works a typical nine to five job and her boss happens to be male, we think her submitting to him is fine. But there is often a particular offense taken (perhaps because of abuse and/or the permanence of the marital relationship) related to submission to a *husband* in our culture.

It is because of this that, when teaching on Ephesians 5, I typically have to slow down and be careful about how people hear and understand this part of the Bible. For this reason, I will be spending four chapters on it.

For this first chapter, my goal is to simply point out that if you read the verse in context, no one (male or female) gets out of submitting. There's more to it than just that, but let me begin there.

The reason I've included verse 18 (which is the beginning of the command "*to be filled by the Spirit*" and is followed by describing what that looks like) and verse 21 (which says Christians are to be "*submitting to one another*") is they flow right into the "offensive" statements in verses 22–24.

It is my belief that verse 21 ("*submitting to one another in the fear of Christ*") is the general command that is given to all Christians. They are to submit to Christ (treat Him like He's more important than you—like He outranks you) by treating other people with submission (treat them like they are more important than you—like *they* outrank you). And I think the next several verses (Ephesians 5:22–6:9) are actually an extended section about *how* to do that in specific relationships.

In the verses that follow Ephesians 5:21, the people with less power *and* the people with more power are given instructions about how to be respectful to the other people in their lives. For instance, children show respect to their parents by obeying them (Ephesians 6:1), and fathers show respect to their children by not stirring up anger in them (Ephesians 6:4). Both sides have to submit to the other in some sense (i.e. elevate the importance of the other person) for the other person's good. But, of course, children and fathers are going to do that in two different ways.

The same goes for husbands and wives. The wife is given a more straightforward submission command here, while the husband is told to show a sacrificial love for his wife the way Jesus did when he died for us—treating the church as if we were more important than Him.

Either way, no one gets out of "submitting" in this portion of the Bible. It just looks different for different people.

Prayer: *Lord, please fill me with Your Spirit so I may submit to You, and therefore submit to everyone else You call me to respect and love.*

SUBMISSION IN MARRIAGE
PART TWO

"...be filled by the Spirit... submitting to one another in the fear of Christ. Wives, submit to your own husbands as to the Lord, for the husband is the head of the wife as Christ is the head of the church. He is the Savior of the body. Now as the church submits to Christ, so wives are to submit to their husbands in everything. Husbands, love your wives, just as Christ loved the church and gave Himself for her."

~Ephesians 5:18b & 21–25

ontinuing on the verses we looked at yesterday, I'd like to now answer a question that often comes up: "Wait a minute. Is this stuff for *nowadays*? I've heard things were crazy back during the time period of the Roman Empire. And so, sure, maybe a wife was supposed to submit to her husband back in *that* culture, but certainly this doesn't apply *anymore*, right?"

We must be careful with this kind of thinking. Firstly, yes, we must admit there are commandments in the Bible that apply to a situation we no longer have, and therefore they must be updated, in principle, to a situation we *do* have.

For instance, when the Bible says "*Dishonest scales are detestable to the Lord*" it is right and good to realize the intention behind that statement (in their culture) and then apply it to contemporary situations.

Thousands of years ago, the Lord was condemning a merchant using a "dishonest scale" so he could charge his customer for one pound of flour and then only give 80% of a pound of flour. That specific verse hardly applies to most Christians nowadays. However, that doesn't mean the verse doesn't matter anymore. We should reason that "dishonest computer programs are *also* detestable to the Lord" and we shouldn't cheat people out of what is rightfully theirs by using modern computer software, either. So, in a sense, yes, some of God's commands have to be "updated" to our current situation.

But please notice the intention of thinking through the command through a modern lens is to actually *obey* the command, not to look for a way to *not obey* it. When Christians say, "that was a long time ago," they need to be careful to think about how the verse applies to our culture, rather than using those words to dismiss God's instructions.

In this case, I don't see how marriage relationships have changed in such a way that we have to think of them like the way we think about the change from analog scales to computer scales.

In fact, just consider the point of the verses that come just before and after the section we usually try to say "isn't for nowadays."

v. 21—Submit to one another
v. 22–24—Wives submit to your husbands
v. 25—Husbands love your wives

I've met plenty of Christians who say the middle command in that list is "not for nowadays" but I don't think I've ever heard any of them say the same thing about the verses just before it and after it. I don't hear people saying, "Submit to one another? Nah, that was for a long time ago. This kind of respect isn't for modern relationships." And I especially have never heard anyone say, "Husbands, love your wives? That was something for back then. No one expects husbands to love their wives anymore."

So when someone chooses to believe the first statement is universal, but then it is followed by an expired/cultural one, but then happens to be followed by another universal one—well, I just think that's a hint we aren't actually trying to follow the Scriptures. We are simply looking for ways to jettison the teachings we don't like, while holding on to the ones we do. But if we do that, who is really the rulemaker—God—in our life?

Prayer: *Almighty God, I do not want to disregard anything You have revealed to me. Help me to understand Your words, and may I try not to use my personal preferences and beliefs as ways to not listen to or obey You.*

Submission In Marriage
Part Three

"...be filled by the Spirit... submitting to one another in the fear of Christ. Wives, submit to your own husbands as to the Lord, for the husband is the head of the wife as Christ is the head of the church. He is the Savior of the body. Now as the church submits to Christ, so wives are to submit to their husbands in everything. Husbands, love your wives, just as Christ loved the church and gave Himself for her."
~Ephesians 5:18b & 21–25

Note: the phrase "submitting to one another in the *fear* of Christ" in this verse doesn't mean "submit because you are *horrified* by Christ" but something more like "submit out of *reverence* for Christ."

$\mathscr{H}$aving established "everyone has to submit in some sense" and "we shouldn't dismiss this as stuff only for way back then," we can now move on to what this passage means. We'll focus on the wife part first, since that one comes first in the passage. Beginning with verse 21 where it says every Christian ought to "*submit to one another in the fear of Christ*" we can see Christians were expected to have a humble attitude toward one another, essentially considering their fellow brothers and sisters to be more important than them. (In fact, those exact instructions are found in Philippians 2:3–5).

The next verses tell wives how to do that toward their husbands. They are to submit to them as the head of their household (just as Christ is the head of the church). The same idea comes up again in verse 33 of that same chapter, but in that case, it says the husband is to "*love his wife as himself, and the wife is to* respect *her husband.*"

Note: These words are translated from a Greek text, so not all translations use the word "respect." The original word used here is the Greek word for "fear." But telling wives to "fear their husbands" doesn't give the correct sense of what was meant, so most translators don't translate it that way. It's talking about something more like reverence or respect for someone who is higher in rank.

The submission spoken of here is not an *absolute* submission. Only God receives absolute submission. Any lesser authority on this earth can only be submitted to in so far as it doesn't displease God as the higher authority.

For instance, if a husband says to his wife, "Hey honey, we are a little low on cash this month. Go steal some money from our next-door neighbors so I can pay the bills." The wife would be obligated to say "No" to her husband out of reverence for God, who has said, "Do not steal." Similarly, this submission doesn't mean women are to endure harm from a husband with no recourse. There are many situations where the criminal justice system can and should step in to remove a husband from a home if he chooses to harm his wife rather than protect her.

Having addressed exceptions, let me end by saying one shouldn't use exceptions as a way to dismiss these commands in their entirety. The submission/respect that is spoken about in these verses is to be taken seriously as God would not have included it in His word if He didn't want it to be applied.

The passage says *"the husband is the head of the wife as Christ is the head of the church."* There is a kind of hierarchy mentioned here, where the wife is expected to show a *he-out-ranks-me* kind of respect toward her husband, as the church submits to her Savior.

It is at this point I can imagine someone saying, "Well, that's not fair! Why doesn't this passage tell husbands to submit to their wives?" And to that I say: "In a way, it does." But we will be getting to that in the next chapter.

Prayer: *Jesus, help me to show submission/respect on all of the many occasions You call for it. May I do this because of the submission and respect I have for You.*

Day 16

Submission In Marriage
Part Four

"...be filled by the Spirit... submitting to one another in the fear of Christ. Wives, submit to your own husbands as to the Lord, for the husband is the head of the wife as Christ is the head of the church. He is the Savior of the body. Now as the church submits to Christ, so wives are to submit to their husbands in everything. Husbands, love your wives, just as Christ loved the church and gave Himself for her."
~Ephesians 5:18b & 21–25

*T*oday we move on to the husband's submission. I'm sorry it has taken me a while to get to it, but I thought it would be worth it to work through this passage slowly and methodically so as not to miss anything important.

It seems to me husbands are included in the command to submit back in verse 21 where it says *"submitting to one another in the fear of Christ."* That command was to everyone. The husbands. The wives. The parents. The children.

However, the verses that come after verse 21 give more specifics about what that looks like in specific situations where there are power differentials. This is a big deal. You wouldn't want an "everyone-is-equal-and-can-fend-for-themselves" kind of policy between two parties of unequal strength. Much of the time, that will lead to injustice toward the weaker parties. Children and wives would get harmed by parents and husbands if there weren't some kind of submissive respect that was also required of the stronger parties. And by the time you get to verse 25, you see the way husbands are supposed to consider their wives as more important than themselves.

Husbands are told to love their wives "*just as Christ loved the church.*" If taken seriously, this should dispel any concern that the Bible allows for husbands to be tyrannical and abusive. Christ was neither tyrannical nor abusive to His church. And He is the example to follow.

And it goes further than that. Ephesians specifies: "*just as Christ loved the church and gave Himself for her,*" which must be a reference to the fact that Christ died (on the cross) for the good of His church. So how far does a husband have to go with sacrificial love? All the way to the point of suffering and death.

My best understanding of this is that the husband is the "head" and the leader of his family, and he is called to value his wife so much (and I assume this would extend to children in the situations that call for it) that if something bad is going to happen, he needs to let it be done to him and not her. If someone has to suffer, let it be the husband and not the wife. If someone has to die, let it be the husband and not the wife.

Because the husband has been assigned Jesus' role in this scenario, we see a humble, submissive, sacrificial love is being required of him for all the days of his marriage. And if this is "unfair" (in the sense that it is unequal) it is tilted not in favor of the husband. The way I see it (because of the analogy of Christ/church; where the church gets the better end of the deal) God requires more from husbands than wives.

In summary: Every Christian should submit to other Christians. In marriage, wifely submission looks like a straightforward he-outranks-me kind of respect as she follows her husband's lead. And the husband's submission is a humble, sacrificial love where he consistently puts his wife's interests ahead of his own, even as he leads their home. And when the people of God do this rightly, we mirror the gospel to the world.

Prayer: *Jesus, thank You for giving Yourself sacrificially for me. Help me to reflect Your gospel in this world.*

Pretend You are Your Spouse's Defense Attorney

> *"Do nothing out of rivalry or conceit, but in humility consider others as more important than yourselves. Everyone should look out not only for his own interests but also for the interests of others."*
>
> ~Philippians 2:3–4

A couple of decades ago, I first heard this piece of marriage advice: "Men, learn to argue her side of the argument." It quickly became a valuable practice in my marriage. I now recommend it to others, though I usually make it unisex by changing it to: "Learn to argue *your spouse's* side of the argument." Another way to say it is: "Pretend you are your spouse's defense attorney."

In my marriage, I am the one who needs this advice more, because I am the one of us who has more of a litigator's personality. (I am more naturally drawn to actions like *persuading* people and *presenting evidence* than my wife is.) However, I can imagine there are other marriages where the wife is the litigator. In those cases, a wife may need this advice more than her husband.

Either way, here is the idea: once an argument starts, pause for a bit and imagine what you might say *to you*, if you were on your spouse's side. (Because, in a marriage, there's a real sense that you actually are on your spouse's side. See chapters three and four of this book.)

This is not natural for most people. Usually, when arguing, each side is mostly concerned with proving themselves to be "right." So we take the role of prosecutor and begin to accuse our spouse of things. Then they take up the role of defender, trying to defend their view while we continue to try to prove them wrong.

All of this is fine for a courtroom. However, in the living room, it has the potential to lead to a joyless marriage. Often, the best "arguer" will win most of the fights, but they will not have really "won" the long game of having a happy marriage.

There is something very powerful that happens when you can summarize your spouse's perspective, and then present it in as compelling of a way as you can. If you do this often enough, you will eventually come across an occasion where you realize you are the one who is wrong. (And the person who out-argued you will be *you!*)

To be clear, the point isn't for you to never win an argument, or for you to never point out your spouse's wrongdoing. There are occasions where pointing out your spouse's wrongdoing is the right thing to do. The point is try to see it from both sides before you continue down a path of accusing and/or defending yourself.

After having practiced this for several years in my own marriage, I wondered if there were any Bible verses that backed it up. And one that came to mind is the passage at the beginning of this chapter.

"Do nothing out of rivalry or conceit" means to not get caught up in self-interest and vainglory, which is what often happens when we become desperate to win a debate. In these situations, *"In humility consider others as more important than yourselves"* means to not think so highly of yourself that you bulldoze over the other person as if they don't matter. And *"Everyone should look out not only for his own interests but also for the interests of others"* makes it clear it's not all about you. So you can afford to take some time to consider what is important to them.

These verses aren't specific to marriage. The Apostle Paul wrote them for a whole congregation of Christians. However, I think they apply well to marriages, and even the particular circumstance of spousal disagreements. I hope this practice helps you as much as it did me.

Prayer: *Lord, please help me to want to win my spouse/friend more than I want to win an argument.*

DAY 18

Husbands, Don't Misuse Your Strength

"Husbands, in the same way, live with your wives with an understanding of their weaker nature yet showing them honor as coheirs of the grace of life, so that your prayers will not be hindered."

~1 Peter 3:7

Unlike yesterday's verses, this verse was given specifically to one gender. This is a marriage verse for husbands from the Apostle Peter.

I believe this verse echoes a concept I mentioned earlier when I said that an "everyone-is-equal-and-can-fend-for-themselves" kind of policy between two parties of unequal strength can lead to injustice. To put it another way: It's not fair to put an 80 lb. child and a 200 lb. child into a room and tell them to "work out their disagreements." That conversation might end with the disagreement resolved because the smaller kid was knocked unconscious.

This Bible verse, while probably offending some people, recognizes men are typically stronger than women. This is certainly true when it comes to physicality. I didn't look up any statistics about bench presses or bicep curls, but a quick internet search reveals the average man in America is five inches taller and thirty pounds heavier than the average woman. I also think most people would also agree men, when compared to women, lean more toward physical aggression when problem-solving.

In addition to this (or perhaps because of this) men also have an advantage over women in other areas. Historically, it has not been uncommon for men to have higher social standing, more non-physical power and influence, and more financial resources than women generally have. Like it or not, this is the world we live in. And some of this (like physical strength and physical aggression) could hardly be changed even if everyone wanted it.

This passage is very helpful though, in that God in some ways takes the woman's side. Notice how the verse ends. The husband needs to be careful how he treats his wife "*so that [his] prayers will not be hindered.*" While I suppose a prayer could be hindered by either party (i.e. a man could choose to not pray OR God could choose not to listen) it seems obvious to me this verse is threatening something on God's behalf. It doesn't seem to me the Apostle Peter was worried the man will stop praying. I think he was saying something more like: "Crush your wife and God will stop listening to you. He won't be on your side."

That is powerful. There is no comparable verse in the Bible I can think of that says God will stop listening to wives' prayers.

The men being addressed here are told to "*live with your wives with an understanding of their weaker nature,*" and that is followed by the instruction to be "*showing them honor as coheirs of the grace of life.*" So the wife is not his equal (physically) and yet he is to honor her as an equal (co-heir).

A husband will, at times, have to hold back, and not take advantage of everything within his power when he lives with his wife. For instance, have you ever seen an argument between a man and a woman where they are *both* screaming at the top their lungs? I don't think God considers that to be a fair fight—at least not in most cases. Even though they are both putting in the same amount of effort, he is scarier and more threatening than her. And it's not right for him to take advantage of that, since she is his equal before God.

Bottom line: A husband should use his strength for his wife's good and never for her harm.

Prayer: *Lord, I recognize that You did not make a world where everyone has the exact same strengths and weaknesses. Help me to not exert power or exploit a weakness in a way that is contrary to Your will. Thank You for listening to my prayers*

CONTENTMENT

*"I rejoiced in the Lord greatly that once again you
renewed your care for me... I don't say this out of need,
for I have learned to be content in whatever circumstances I am. I know both how to have a little and I
know how to have a lot... I am able to do all things
through Him who strengthens me."*
~Philippians 4:10a, 11–12a, and 13

This is one of the most helpful passages found in the New
Testament regarding the topic of contentment. Unfortu-
nately, verse 13 (the most famous portion) is usually quoted
out of context so most people don't even know the verse is
about contentment.

I've seen the words *"I can do all things through Christ who
gives me strength"* on weightlifting belts, dri-fit tank tops, and
volleyball awards. Christians just love to connect this verse
to athletic achievements. Having a hard time getting your
mile run under seven minutes? Don't worry: Philippians 4:13.
Jesus will help you run.

Now, don't get me wrong. I believe Jesus has all authority
in heaven and on earth. If He wants you to run a six-minute
mile, you will. But that's not what the verse is about. I think

71

people just got excited when they saw the combination "I can do all things" (where it sounds like they are accomplishing an incredible task) with the word "strength" (with an assumption it's about physical strength).

In context (and even in the abbreviated version I have above) you can tell the verse actually means: I can endure all circumstances and keep my contentment intact, because of my spiritual connection to Jesus. I suppose that sounds less impressive than bench-pressing 300 lbs, but it's more important.

This is another one of those verses that isn't specific to marriage. It's actually a thank you note from the Apostle Paul to the Philippians for a gift (probably money) they sent him when he was imprisoned for his faith. He was telling them he was happy to receive it ("*I rejoiced in the Lord greatly*") but he didn't need it in order to be happy ("*I don't say this out of need, for I have learned to be content.*")

It is helpful for us to know this kind of contentment is possible. There were times Paul was well-fed and had a lot going for him, and there were times (like this occasion in prison) where he had very little, and things weren't as good as they used to be. Either way, Jesus gave him inner strength to be content with the life he'd been given.

Sometimes single people are discontent that they are not married. Sometimes married people are discontent that they are not single. Sometimes discontentment shows up even in the good times when everything seems to be going well. Often discontentment shows up when things go south, and the situation isn't as good as it was last year.

In this passage, Paul is saying in any and all of those situations, a contentment is available from God to the person who trusts in Him. Therefore, I've included this passage in this book for anyone in a difficult marriage, or in a difficult time of singleness. Through a relationship with Jesus (more on that in chapters 29 & 30) one can be strengthened for contentment in whatever circumstances they find themselves in.

Prayer: *Jesus, I ask that You would provide me with the inner strength I need to be content, even as I go through difficult circumstances.*

CELIBACY FOR UNMARRIED PEOPLE
SEX FOR MARRIED PEOPLE

"Now in response to the matters you wrote about: 'It is good for a man not to have relations with a woman.' But because sexual immorality is so common, each man should have his own wife, and each woman her own husband."

~1 Corinthians 7:1–2

With the possible exception of the verses we learned on days 13–16 of this book, the concept found in these verses might be the most out-of-step with our current culture in America. The idea that sexual activity between a man and a woman should not begin until *after* they have had their wedding has not been in vogue at any point during my lifetime.

However, the exact timing of when sexual activity ought to begin in a relationship has differed over the four decades that I have been alive. I would say when I was growing up ('80s–'90s) the cultural expectation was that you ought to wait until you were "in love" before you had sex with someone. However, most of my adulthood (let's say from the year 2000 until now) I would say that expectation has changed to be something more like "you have sex after one to four dates" regardless of anyone having to love anyone.

As you can tell, the expectation assumed in the Bible is very different from this. In the above verses, celibacy was assumed as a good and appropriate thing for people who were not yet married. I think that's why there is a commendation of the phrase, *'It is good for a man not to have relations with a woman.'* However, it was understood that it's not likely to be God's will that all of them be celibate forever and so the alternative was clear: marriage.

Over the next few chapters, we will discuss some of the reasons why this is the case, but before we get into the *why*, I figured it would be good to lay down the *what*. The Bible assumes sexual relations were for two people who had committed their whole lives to one another.

Here the Apostle Paul is writing a response letter to the Christians in the city of Corinth. Apparently they had asked him about sex because this section of the letter begins with the words: *"Now in response to the matters you wrote about…"*

At the time of writing this, Paul was an unmarried and celibate man, and he had no problem recommending singleness and celibacy to his fellow brothers and sisters. He does this in verse 8 of this same chapter. As crazy as celibacy might sound to some people, a review of the chapter on contentment might be helpful. Yes, people can live good lives apart from sex. Even Jesus did it.

However, Paul also mentioned it would be better for people to get married than to *"burn with passion"* (verse 9 of this same chapter). And it's important to notice the proposed solution. He doesn't say, "Since sexual immorality is so common, go ahead and have sex after one to four dates."

He doesn't even say "Wait until you are 'in love' and then go for it." He assumes the same thing that is assumed all over the Scriptures when it comes to sex: "*each man should have his own wife, and each woman her own husband.*"

I believe God has good reasons for this standard which we will get to. But for now, let us simply take in that God's word is clear and countercultural: Sex is for people who are married to each other.

Prayer: *Lord, help me to understand what You have revealed about sexuality. Also, help me to be poised to obey You, even before I understand all of Your reasons.*

DAY 21

SEX CAUSES SOME KIND OF UNION

"Don't you know that your bodies are a part of Christ's body? So should I take a part of Christ's body and make it part of a prostitute? Absolutely not! Don't you know that anyone joined to a prostitute is one body with her? For Scripture says, 'the two will become one flesh.'"

~1 Corinthians 6:15–16

*T*oday, we see a portion of the New Testament that quotes the portion of the Old Testament we looked at on day three of this book. In this case, the phrase *"the two will become one flesh"* which we know is about marriage (Jesus used it in his answer to a question about divorce) is applied to the topic of sex. That's important to catch; the Bible closely identifies sexual activity with marriage.

In this case, the reasoning is that there is some kind of union involved with sexual behavior. The author (Paul) asks: *"Don't you know that anyone joined to a prostitute is one body with her?"* and *"Should I take a part of Christ's body and make it part of a prostitute?"*

Why would it be when the body of a Christ-follower engages in sexual activity with a prostitute (this may be a reference to a temple prostitute; pagan religions at the time commonly used sex as a religious practice) it would be considered that part of Christ is being united to that prostitute?

It is because faith in Christ is a union-causing activity (it connects us to Christ) and sex is also a union-causing activity (it connects us to that other person).

In fact, someone who doesn't even believe the Bible might find this concept easy to accept. After all, sex brings people together in ways other activities do not; there are reasons we are willing to shake hands with a lot more people than we are willing to have sex with. And there are reasons people often regret sleeping with someone (when they look back on their past) but they rarely regret hugging or high-fiving someone.

Years ago, I used to lead a ministry to high school students, and I remember noticing times when a female student would break up with a boyfriend who treated her poorly. I'd think, "Good for you, girl. Drop him. He's not good for you." But oftentimes, a week or two later they would be back together. I'd wonder, why do these girls stick with these guys who treat them like dirt? Sometimes the answer is: because they are sleeping together. There is a kind of union that has taken place, and she's having a hard time breaking it off.

Yes, that's what sex does. It unites two people in a special way. And that's why people who haven't made their relationship permanent *shouldn't* do it, and why people who have made a life-long commitment to one another *should* do it.

As much as it goes against our current culture's practices, it makes sense that a good Father would tell His children to not do a union-causing activity with someone who they should not be united to, and why He would tell His children to engage in a union-causing activity in the cases where He wants them to stay together for life.

It also makes sense why Paul would tell the Corinthians (both married and single) that connecting yourself to a temple prostitute (through sex) is dishonoring to the Savior to whom you have connected your whole life.

Prayer: *Jesus, may I consider that my body belongs to You first and foremost. I pray You would guide me to take what belongs to You and use it in a way that is consistent with what You intend.*

SEX IS FOR PROCREATION

"So God created man in His own image; He created him in the image of God; He created them male and female. God blessed them, and God said to them, 'Be fruitful, multiply, fill the earth, and subdue it.'"

~Genesis 1:27–28a

Yesterday's chapter covered one of the things sex does: causes union. Today we move on to another thing sex does: causes people. A person could have very little Bible knowledge and only a basic understanding of biology and know that sex is the primary mechanism that causes the procreation of humanity.

On the first page, the Bible describes God creating males and females, and records Him giving a command that the two sexes could only accomplish together. (We touched on this on day four.) The mission was for them to make more people—so humanity would rule the world. It is obvious sex plays a big role in this.

And this also brings us to another reason sex was intended for married people. God created a system: As new humans came into the world, they would (ideally) have one person from each sex helping them to survive, guiding them toward adulthood, and preparing them for God's will on this earth.

Prior to the advent of birth control pills and other modern contraceptives, humans understood that to have a sexual relationship with someone greatly increased the likelihood you would produce children with that person. So there was a built-in reason to be careful who you had sex with.

Sure, birth control changed the likelihood of that happening in the cases where it is not desired, but contraceptives did not change:

- All of the occasions when contraceptives fail to do what they were designed to do
- God's original intention for sexuality
- The fact that sex causes some kind of union even apart from childbearing.

God's plan for sex (particularly human sex) in His creation is that it would exist alongside another institution called parenting. God didn't simply want people to only multiply numerically. He wanted the older people to protect, sustain, and train up the younger people so they would turn out a particular way. We see places all over the Scripture (Deuteronomy 6:5–7, Exodus 12:26–27, Proverbs 22:6, Luke 11:11–12, Ephesians 6:4 are just five examples) that either say or assume this.

There's a connection between sex and marriage. There's a connection between sex and parenting. And, therefore, there's a connection between marriage and parenting. We can see God intended for sex to be shared between two people who'd made a life-long commitment to one another and who typically would also be making a long-term commitment to a portion of the next generation of humans (the ones they brought into the world). God intended for sex to be a way that His people obey Him and run the world according to His will and glory.

Prayer: *Father, people often overlook, forget, or are ignorant of what You intended for Your creation. Guide me, that I may cooperate with Your plan. This includes my sexual and parenting choices.*

Day 23

A Quick Primer on Parenting

"Sons are indeed a heritage from the Lord, children, a reward."
~Psalm 127:3

"Love the Lord your God will all your heart… these words that I am giving you today are to be in your heart. Repeat them to your children."
~Deuteronomy 6:5a & 6–7a

"Foolishness is tangled up in the heart of a youth; the rod of discipline will drive it away from him."
~Proverbs 22:15

"Fathers, do not exasperate your children, so they won't become discouraged."
~Colossians 3:21

*H*aving brought up the topic of parenting in the previous chapter, it seemed good to me to include a chapter on the basics of parenting. After all, that is one of the biggest issues married couples deal with. However, I also realized there is so much to say (people write whole books on this topic!), and this is supposed to be a book on *marriage* and not on *parenting*. So I am limiting myself to four brief passages and four brief points and spending just one paragraph on each. The passages are above, and here are the points:

1. Children are from God and are considered to be a blessing.
2. Parents should bring their children up to love and obey God.
3. Raising children includes discipline.
4. Parents should not abuse their authority.

Point #1: Psalm 127:3 states that children are a gift from God. This is an important truth to remember since we live in a society where many people treat children as if they are a curse. I can't remember the number of times—when I was in the first years of my marriage and I would tell people about how I enjoyed my life with my wife—they would say in an ominous tone of voice, "Just wait until you have children." Well, yes, it turned out raising children was more difficult than not raising them. However, an attitude of treating children like they are a punishment from God makes parenting more difficult. Pretend you are a child; who would you rather be raised by? Parents who believe you are a blessing from God? Or parents who believe you are a curse to be endured?

Point #2: Deuteronomy 6:5–7 commands parents to teach their children to love God. This is a tough one, because you can't ultimately control whether or not your children choose to trust in and follow after God. But you do have the opportunity to teach them by your words and by your example. I've noticed my children love a lot of the same things I love (foods, housing, vacation activities), and in many cases, they love those things because *I* loved them first. Never forget that. Some of you reading this book will have children who grow up to love the Creator of the universe, because you loved Him first.

Point #3: Proverbs 22:15 teaches that kids are not naturally bent toward wisdom and righteousness but rather that "*foolishness*" is "*tangled up*" in their hearts. (It may be helpful to know Proverbs often uses the word "foolishness" and "unrighteousness" synonymously.) According to the verse, a primary way to fix this foolishness is discipline. Introducing some unpleasantness into the life of our children when they do wrong things is good for them. They will benefit from associating the unpleasantness with the bad behavior. Some parents are hesitant to bring any kind of negative consequence into the life of their child, but to not drive our children away from unrighteousness is not being loving toward them (see also Proverbs 13:24).

Point #4: Colossians 3 instructs fathers to "not exasperate" their children. Other words for exasperate include embitter, provoke, and aggravate. Obviously, there will be times when a child is aggravated by the discipline recommended in Proverbs 22:15. I don't think that's what this verse is referring to. I think the idea is to not mistreat your children in such a way that you break their spirit and cause them to lose heart (the passage says "*so they won't become discouraged.*") Parents have a lot of power over the lives of their children, and they should be sure to treat them the way they would want to be treated (see Luke 6:31) and to never neglect or abuse them.

Prayer: *God, what You have revealed about parenting is more important than my personal opinions about parenting. Conform me to Your will and desires. Please give me wisdom as I have to navigate thousands of decisions over the course of my life. I'm sure I won't get them all right, but I do want to walk in Your ways.*

Tell the Truth

*"Since you put away lying, speak the truth each one
to his neighbor, because we are members of one another."*
~Ephesians 4:25

We are approaching the conclusion of this book, and for many of these final chapters we will focus on Ephesians 4:25–5:2. Leading up to these verses, Paul told these early followers of Jesus to not live *"your former way of life"* but to *"put on the new self, the one created according to God's likeness in righteousness and purity of truth."*

I must admit these teachings (covered in the next several chapters) were not specifically written for married people, nor are they addressing only marriage. This section of God's word is full of instructions about how all Christians are supposed to communicate with one another.

This is good for two reasons. First of all, this means it doesn't matter if you are divorced, married with kids, married with no kids, or never been married; all of these verses are for you. You can allow them to guide how to communicate with your co-workers, or your extended family, or the people in your church (in fact, verses 25 and 32 make it clear this passage is especially about Christian-to-Christian relationships).

The second reason this is good is that these verses, though not exclusively about marriage, *do* apply to marriage. In fact, if one believer marries another believer, then all of the Christian-to-Christian relational Bible verses would apply to their marriage.

So, on to the first one. Ephesians 4:25 says "*Speak the truth each one to his neighbor, because we are members of one another.*" I believe this is one of the best places to begin when discussing marital communication: Tell the truth.

This, of course, can be expressed in the negative as well: Do not lie. In fact, the verse does phrase it both ways: "*Since you put away lying, speak the truth each one to his neighbor...*"

As a married person, you must not lie to your spouse. There are very few things you can do to cause more long-term damage to your marriage than to get to the point that your spouse has good reason not to trust you. Even if it's embarrassing, even if it's uncomfortable, we must not lie to each other if we want to build a healthy marriage. Once a husband doesn't believe the words that come out of his wife's mouth (or vice-versa) many other forms of communication (apologies, requests for forgiveness, explanations, acts of gratitude, repentance, recommitments) become meaningless and/or powerless.

In fact, it's helpful to see this verse gives a motivation for telling the truth: "*because we are members of one another.*" Like I said above, this verse was written to a group of Christians who would have considered themselves to be partners and spiritual family members to one another. The reason given for avoiding lying is that it is self-sabotage; you are harming people on your own team. This is doubly true for married Christians who lie. You are harming yourself by harming the person you've united to.

If you've already started the habit, here's my advice (from personal experience) for how to move away from lying. Whenever you catch yourself in a lie, confess it (on your own, without having to get caught) and then tell the truth as soon as you remember to do so. At first, it may take several minutes or an hour. You'll say something false (out of habit) and then think back on it and realize it's not true. So you go back to the person you lied to and say, "I'm sorry, I said _____ which is not true. I should have said _____." If it works in your life the way it worked in mine, here's what will happen next: The amount of time that passes between the lie and the confession will get shorter and shorter. Eventually, it will move from five minutes to one minute. And then after that, it will move from one minute to five seconds. After a while, the truth will start coming out of your mouth immediately after the lie. When the process is complete, the truth will come out of your mouth *before* the lie, and therefore the lie won't come out at all.

There's no Bible verse for this strategy that I am aware of. That's just personal advice that worked for me. And, of course, this advice will only work for people who actually desire to stop lying. Your motivations in all of this truly matter a lot. *"Since you put away lying, speak the truth each one to his neighbor, because we are members of one another."*

Prayer: *Thank You for being a God of truth. Please help me to put away falsehood.*

DON'T STAY ANGRY

"Be angry and do not sin. Don't let the sun go down on your anger."

~Ephesians 4:26

This verse comes directly after yesterday's verse about lying. That is because, as mentioned yesterday, this verse is found in a list of behaviors Christians are supposed to do (and many of them are specific ways Christians are supposed to communicate). This part of the list is about not holding grudges.

A few years ago, I wrote a book on the topic of handling conflict, and I quoted this verse. At the time, I mentioned that even though that book wasn't a book on marriage, this verse is often quoted to married people to help them to remember to not sleep in separate beds on the evenings they are mad at each other, but rather to try to work it out before the day is done. I also mentioned since this verse isn't specifically written to married people, it applies to unmarried people too.

All of that is still true, but I will re-write some things I said then for the benefit of anybody reading this book who didn't get a chance to read that one.

This verse is practical in that it is one of the few places in the Bible that makes it clear you can be angry and yet not sin. (Other places would include the narratives that speak about Jesus being angry. Since we know He never sinned, and yet he got angry on occasion, we can know that anger is not automatically always sinful.) However, the fact the verse even combines anger and sin the way it does reveals the underlying assumption that it's often easy to be angry in sinful ways.

The second half of the verse is also helpful. "*Don't let the sun go down on your anger*" is a figure of speech that, while not forbidding anger entirely, tells the person not to *stay* angry. Apparently, we shouldn't bring yesterday's anger into today, and we shouldn't bring today's anger into tomorrow.

This is a helpful reminder to not stew on an offense for a long time, doing nothing to fix it other than allowing bitterness to grow. This happens in marriages quite often. As someone who has done a fair bit of marriage counseling, I've witnessed multiple conversations where one spouse complains about something that happened recently, and the other spouse, in response, brings up something from years earlier. And as a third-party observer it's quite clear that spouse #2 either never addressed, or never forgave, that sin from years ago.

"*Don't let the sun go down on your anger*" is a wise motivational statement for us. It's not always wrong to be offended, but the time to take care of it is near the time it happened. We should not let anger fester for long periods of time. That goes against the Bible (and is therefore wrong), but it is also impractical. It's harder to deal with issues once a lot of time has gone by.

Prayer: *Lord, I ask for wisdom. Help me to bring up the things that ought to be addressed, and help me to overlook and/or forgive the things that I need to get over.*

Use Words to Build up Rather Than Tear Down

"No foul language is to come from your mouth, but only what is good for building up someone in need, so that it gives grace to those who hear."

~Ephesians 4:29

Oh, what a wonderful verse; if only everyone would obey it! And yet, before we apply this verse to our lives, I think we should first address the words translated: *"foul language."* What does that mean?

It turns out there are multiple ways the Greek words (logos and sapros) have been translated over the years. The version of the Bible I use most often says: *"foul language"* but other translations include the phrases: *"unwholesome talk,"* *"rotten word,"* and *"corrupt communication."* Side-by-side, it's plain to see those phrases are all synonymous. However, for some reason, to me, the words *"foul language"* seem to be a lot more specific than the other translations. Maybe it's just the area of the country I grew up in, but the phrase "foul language" was always (in my childhood) used to describe a list of words (I suppose there were about six or seven of them) people weren't supposed to say if they wanted to be considered kind and polite. Whereas the ideas brought up by the other translations (like "*corrupt communication*") seem to indicate a kind of evil talk that would be much broader than a short list of curse words.

I don't have a problem with the translation saying "*foul language*," however, it would be a shame if someone took this Scripture to merely mean: "Don't cuss."

Perhaps this verse does forbid cussing as we define it. But even if it does, it's got to be way bigger than that. The second half of the verse reveals that. The words that are being forbidden are contrasted with words that "*build up*" and "*give grace*."

I can admit there have been occasions where I certainly tore someone down with my words, without ever using a cuss word. You probably have too. And when I think of the words that have hurt me most in my life, they usually didn't include any cuss words at all. Even if we rid our marriages of the seven words that HBO *can* use but NBC *can't* use, that would not necessarily mean we are using our words only for the good of our spouse and never for their harm.

Additionally, this "*so that it gives grace to those who hear*" requirement means our standard of what to say cannot be simply determined by the question, "Is it true?" Yes, saying true things is important (remember chapter 24?), but not every true thing needs to be said out loud.

Some of you with certain personality types need to re-read that last sentence: Not every true thing needs to be said out loud.

Sometimes I have seen children (even one of my own) taunt each other while playing games together. They will say things like "Ha ha! I won; you lost! I'm better at this than you!" And when I have rebuked one of my children for speaking that way, it wasn't because they were lying. After all, it was *true* that they won, and the other kid lost. Yet, I told them to stop talking that way. Why? Because the words were not said to "*build up*" or to "*give grace.*" It was not helpful communication.

This doesn't change once we get older. In marriage, we can't merely settle for statements that are free of cuss words and falsehoods. We need to make sure the motive behind our speech is to help our spouse and not to harm them.

This doesn't mean spouses aren't allowed to bring up topics their partner doesn't want to hear. Sometimes it is good to have awkward conversations to get to the bottom of an issue. But even in those times, the goal of the speech must be to help and not to harm.

Prayer: *Father, help me to determine the things You would like me to say and help me to keep my mouth shut when I have words that shouldn't be said. Holy Spirit, please guide me to have the right motives when I talk.*

LESS SHOUTING

"All bitterness, anger and wrath, shouting and slan-
der must be removed from you, along with all malice."
~Ephesians 4:31

 itterness. Anger. Wrath. Shouting. Slander. Malice.
These are all qualities we don't want in our marriages, and
these are ways that we ought not communicate with our
loved ones. We already covered bitterness and anger in Day
25 and will return to them on Day 28, so let us now focus
on shouting and slander.

To some people, shouting might be the most surprising
thing on this list: Wait? What? It's a sin to shout? Shouting
is on the same level as slander and malice?

Well, of course not all shouting is like that. Elizabeth
shouted something happy to Mary in Luke 1:41–42 and that
passage says she was filled with the Holy Spirit as she did it.
And we can look at the other words in this list and quickly
surmise the Bible is not forbidding the shouting of phrases
like, "Watch out for that bear! He might try to eat you!" or
"Get out of the road! A semi-truck is headed this way!" This is
about raging outbursts, a kind of communication that almost
never helps a marriage (see James 1:20).

I grew up in a family that shouted all the time. We were an excitable bunch, and people would raise their voices even on occasions when they were only mildly angry. It was a bit of a culture-shock when I married my wife and found out she grew up in a family that believed shouting was a special ability God gave us to use only for emergencies.

The first year of our marriage was rough when it came to this issue. I raised my voice far more often than my wife was used to, and it shut her down in ways I didn't understand. At first I thought we simply had two different upbringings and therefore two different preferences—preferences that were both equally good ways of communicating.

Over time I figured out they are not equally good ways of communicating. Some family cultures are better than others, and husbands and wives can't merely "meet in the middle" on everything they disagree on. In this case, I needed to move much farther over to her side than she needed to move my way. "Screaming is for emergencies" really is the better way to go.

Slander is another word in this passage, and it seems related to shouting. It's a kind of evil-speaking that is sometimes translated blasphemy (when it's directed to God) but shows up as slander when it is in reference to other humans.

It's important to make sure we don't use words to tear down the reputation of our spouse, neither when they are around, nor behind their back. Regularly bad-mouthing your spouse is a quick way to pave the road for an affair.

Today's verses are a reminder of, and a more specific application of, the words that had just come earlier in the chapter. We must use words that are *only what is good for building up someone.* If your family must walk on eggshells when you are around because they never know when a raging outburst or a railing against their reputation might erupt, it will not build up anything. That kind of unpredictability wreaks havoc on a family.

Prayer: *Jesus, as I endeavor to love my spouse the way I love myself, and the way You love me, help me to set aside any raising of my voice for the special occasions You made the ability for. Help me to use my words to build up and not to harm.*

DAY 28

FORGIVENESS

"And be kind and compassionate to one another, forgiving one another, just as God also forgave you in Christ."

~Ephesians 4:32

My wife and I have a policy in our marriage we call "The Sixty-Year Grace Period." The idea is if one of us sins against the other one, and the offender repents and asks for forgiveness, the offended party will automatically grant forgiveness for the first sixty years of our marriage. This policy is a bit tongue-in-cheek as we don't expect one day (in our eighties) to begin to keep records of each other's faults and start withholding forgiveness then.

I figure this kind of understatement is acceptable, after all, Jesus once told Peter (Matt. 18:22) to extend forgiveness to other people seventy-seven times (some translations interpret it to be 490 times). Either number you go with, it looks like Jesus gave a specific number when He really meant for us to keep on forgiving indefinitely.

This commitment to forgiveness is so important for marriage. Marriage can be defined many ways (see days 2–6 of this book) but one additional way it can be defined is: Two sinners living under the same roof for life. Under those conditions, it is inevitable that one spouse will offend the other spouse. It is guaranteed. Any arrangement where two sinners are involved is going to have to incorporate forgiveness in order to work long-term. We cannot—we must not—fall for the idea that a healthy marriage is a marriage where the husband and wife never sin against each other. Such marriages do not exist.

Today's passage fits well with what we learned on Day 25. You can be angry, but you shouldn't stay angry. It's not always a sin to take offense (although some people are too easily provoked; see 1 Cor. 13:5), but it is wrong to not let go of an offense when forgiveness should be offered.

We also see the model and motivation for forgiveness mentioned in this verse: *"just as God also forgave you in Christ."*

I say "model" because God showed us how to forgive in sending Jesus to die on the cross for our sins. Jesus paid the price for our sins, and for all those who trust in Him, God does not hold their sins against them. As our role-model in this area, we should follow God's example. There will be times when we must pay the price for the sins of our spouse (often this means absorbing the hurt that was done without exacting punishment/taking revenge) and then no longer hold their sins against them.

I say "motivation" because it is God's forgiveness of us that points us to forgive others. People who have been forgiven of so much, are expected to be forgivers (Jesus made this clear in Matthew 18:32–33). I've heard it said, "Forgiven people must be forgiving people."

Prayer: *Father, please forgive me of my many sins. And help me to extend Your forgiveness to others.*

THE GOSPEL
PART ONE

"Therefore, be imitators of God, as dearly loved children. And walk in love, as the Messiah also loved us and gave Himself for us, a sacrificial and fragrant offering to God."

~Ephesians 5:1–2

*H*ere we have the next two verses that come directly after the verse about forgiveness in yesterday's reading. These verses reiterate the point that our forgiveness and love of others (including the forgiveness and love of our spouse) is an act of following an example that came before us. The person we are to imitate is God. We, as His children, are to be like our Father.

It is also interesting that imitating God is immediately followed, in this passage, by the idea of imitating the Messiah, as if there isn't even a big difference between imitating God and imitating Jesus. This matches up with the passages we looked at back on the first day of this book, when Jesus is used almost interchangeably with "God" as the person by whom and for whom the whole world was made.

We are to imitate both God and the Messiah (who is

God in a body; see Colossians 2:9). Clearly the passage above says we are to be both "*imitators of God,*" and we are to "*walk in love as the Messiah also loved us.*"

This brings us to the most important message in the Bible: the gospel. After all, it is only the good news of Jesus Christ that makes sense of what is said next in these verses. This passage specifies *how* the Messiah loved us—by giving Himself as an offering—but it doesn't get into a lot of details. However, it is obviously a reference to some other story about Jesus that was documented somewhere. What was the author of this passage referring to when he said our love should be an imitation of the Messiah giving Himself as an offering?

Well, if you are a Christian reading this, you likely already know the long version of that story is found in the final chapters of the gospels of Matthew, Mark, Luke, and John—the story of the crucifixion (and resurrection) of Jesus Christ. Additionally, shorter references to that story (along with helpful applications to our own lives) are found all over the books of the Bible that come after those gospels. This is one of those occasions.

The Bible tells the story of how we (all of humanity) have sinned against God and what God (and Jesus) did to bring about the forgiveness and reconciliation that would be needed if we were ever to be made eternally right with God and not be eternally judged for our sins. Here's a run-down:

The Bible makes it clear sin is bad and must be punished. Even if you aren't a Bible-believer, you probably intuitively sense this is true, at least during the occasions when some-one sins against *you.* Those times when we are victimized by others are the times it is most obvious to us there are some behaviors that are truly evil, and something ought to be done about them. God feels the same way. In fact, He believed it before we did.

Additionally, those of us being honest with ourselves would admit there are even occasions when *we* have done the very things we call "wrong"—things we believe ought to be punished when they are done by other people. In fact, if we were to put up a record of our behaviors against God's law in the Bible, we'd see we fall very short very often. (Though this isn't a book on the laws of God, perhaps there were even passages in it that convicted you, in the sense that you realized you did not measure up to God's standards.)

So, what would a holy and just God do about such evil when He finds it in us? It must be punished. In fact, the Bible is clear that if someone dies with their sins unforgiven the result is judgement/Hell.

In the Old Testament, there were offerings that were made to God in order to address the problem of sin. However, even the Bible acknowledges (see Hebrews 10:4) animal sacrifices, on behalf of a human sinner, couldn't truly be the way sins are atoned for.

Here is where the Messiah, Jesus, enters into the picture. The Bible says God offered Him as a sacrifice in our place (see Romans 3:25–26). A perfect human was offered as a *"fragrant and sacrificial offering to God"* in the place of sinners. The sins of everyone who would ever believe in Jesus were paid for when He was punished for them on the cross.

This is good news (for sinners who want to be forgiven), and we will continue to address this (and our reaction to it) in the next chapter.

Prayer: *Jesus, I recognize I am a sinner (maybe for the first time, or maybe for the thousandth time). I praise You for sacrificing Yourself as a perfect offering to take care of the problem of sin.*

THE GOSPEL
PART TWO

"Now brothers, I want to clarify for you the gospel I proclaimed to you; you received it and have taken your stand on it. You are also saved by it, if you hold to the message I proclaimed to you—unless you believe for no purpose. For I passed on to you as most important what I also received: that Christ died for our sins according to the Scriptures, that He was buried, that He was raised according to the Scriptures…"

~1 Corinthians 15:1–4

This is one of my favorite Bible passages. Not only is it on the most important topic in the Bible (notice the passage itself calls this message "*most important*") but it is also one of the clearest sections of the Bible as to what the gospel is and what to do about it. According to these verses the gospel is the message that includes "*that Christ died for our sins*" and "*He was raised.*" We already addressed that Christ died for our sins in yesterday's reading (ie: when Jesus died on the cross, He was giving His life as an offering to pay the consequences of what our sins deserve). However, we haven't yet addressed the part that says "*He was raised according to the Scriptures.*"

Among other things, Jesus' resurrection shows that the Father accepted His sacrifice on our behalf. I suppose anyone could say they are going to "die for you" and then go out and end up dead by the end of the day. But how would you know their death truly has any connection to your life and your sin? God's resurrection of Jesus Christ is the proof that Jesus' and His Apostles' claims were true, and proof that His death worked—that He really died "*for our sins*" as the verses say. The Bible promises eternal life with God for those who believe as a result of the forgiveness we receive in Christ (see John 3:16). We can see eternal life is an actual thing Jesus has. (I can accept my death will be undone one day if the message comes from Someone whose death *was* undone.)

Another thing I love about today's passage is that it says what to do with this information. Notice the Bible says "*You are also saved by it, if you hold to the message.*" Apparently, the action that activates this information is believing it. Trusting it. Knowing it to be true. In fact, the other verb-heavy phrases in this passage ("*you received it*" and you "*have taken your stand on it*") also show what a person's relationship ought to be to the message of Jesus Christ. I guess there are a lot of different ways to say it, but the overall point is that a person needs to not only *hear* Jesus died for their sins and rose again; a person needs to *trust* in Him—believe in who He is and what He accomplished with His life, death, and resurrection.

How do you know if you really believe it? The short answer (one could write a whole book on just this point!) is that you live as if it's true. You live as if Jesus is the Christ (God's anointed King) and submit your whole life to Him. A lot of people say they believe Jesus died for their sins, but they do not live as if He truly is their Lord. To truly "take your stand" on Jesus is to treat Him as He is, the Creator of Heaven and Earth, and the One worthy of our everything.

At this point, you might think I have gotten way off the main topic of this book. What does any of this have to do with marriage? I'll be getting to that in our final chapter.

Prayer: *Lord, thank You for the gospel. I want to always submit to You and Your message.*

WHAT DOES THE GOSPEL
HAVE TO DO WITH MARRIAGE?

*"Now as the church submits to Christ, so wives are
to submit to their husbands in everything. Husbands,
love your wives, just as Christ loved the church and
gave himself up for her to make her holy, cleansing her
with the washing of water by the word. He did this to
present the church to Himself in splendor, without spot
or wrinkle or anything like that, but holy and blameless."*
~*Ephesians 5:24–27*

There is a connection between the most important message in the Bible (the gospel of Jesus Christ) and our main topic of this book (marriage). In fact, it's so clear someone could merely skim the above passage and still see the connection. Marriage mirrors the gospel.

When the Bible describes all of God's people, saved by Jesus, living in eternity, it is occasionally described as a marriage (see 1 Corinthians 11:2 and Revelation 19:6–8). I think this language is somewhat metaphorical, since all of Jesus' people (a huge group) end up as one "bride" connected to Him forever. But the love and care Jesus will forever show His people is very real. Our eternity (those who follow Jesus) is likened to a marriage with accompanying celebration.

Additionally, passages like the one above show that earthly marriages, when done right, are supposed to mirror the big love story between Jesus and His people. Many of the verses covered in this book (particularly the ones from days 2, 13, 14, 15, 16, 21, and 28) point to the idea that we are to use Jesus' relationship with His church as the model for how to operate in our earthly marriages.

This idea—marriages are to be reflections of Christ's relationship to His people—heightens the importance of marriage. Let me repeat something I said toward the beginning of this book: "if marriage is supposed to mirror the relationship Jesus Christ has with His people, then, at the very least, this means we don't just get to make up our own rules about it and govern over it however we want. Marriage is something that is supposed to look and be a particular way, as prescribed by the Creator of it."

I'd also like to point out that there is no way for a person to mirror (in their earthly marriage) an eternal relationship they don't understand or have no part in. I suppose I am saying a person must be rightly committed to Jesus in order to be rightly committed to marriage.

Yes, I'm sure someone can keep most or all of their wedding vows (avoiding adultery, being kind and loving for many decades) apart from being a Christian. But I don't see how a woman can submit to her husband as to the Lord, or how a man can love his wife as Christ loved the church, in the proper way and with the proper motive apart from God.

In order to participate in marriage the way God has designed it, we would need to be:

- familiar with His story of saving us
- aware that we are to reflect that story

- released from the sins that would destroy such a reflection
- empowered/strengthened by God in order to follow His ways in it.

I am ending this book with two different prayers for two different types of people:

Prayer #1: (for someone who is already a Jesus-follower) *Lord, I praise You for including so much about marriage in the Bible. Please help me to own the verses in this book as my possessions—that they would be a part of my life. In particular, I ask You to help me with [insert the Bible passage in this book that was most important to you here.] May I honor You in the way I live my life, and I thank You for the salvation that comes from the gospel of Jesus.*

Prayer #2: (for someone who has not been a Jesus-follower up to this point but now wants to be) *Lord, my eyes are opened more than they have been in the past. I realize I have fallen short of Your standards for my life. I am a sinner and I am sorry. I do not desire to travel any further down the path I have been on. I understand I deserve judgment for my sins, but I now also understand that in Your message, You have described a way of escape from judgment through forgiveness in Jesus Christ—because of His death and resurrection. I trust in You, Jesus. I love You, Jesus. And I now want to love others the way You love me. Please save me. Save me eternally, but also save me in this life that I may live for You—the One who created me.*

Note: If you prayed prayer #2, you should try your best to find a Bible-believing church in your area and get involved there, because this is the beginning of a journey, and you'll need the support of some mature believers as you decide on your next steps.

About the Author

Mario Villella grew up in Ocala, Florida. He spent his early adult years as a youth minister in Rockwall, Texas, and Leesburg, Florida. A graduate of the University of Texas at Dallas with a degree in arts and performance, Mario has been involved in educational and community theater, teaching acting to students, and performing in plays like *The Comedy of Errors*, *The Sound of Music*, *Oliver!*, and *Beauty and the Beast*.

In 2011, he moved back to Ocala and started Good News Church with his wife, Heidi. They have three children. He has written two other books titled, *Working Our Way Through Life* and *It Takes Two to Tangle*.

Mario's sermons can be viewed at Good News Church Ocala on YouTube.